The aMAZEing voyage of...
CHARLES DARWIN

ANNA NILSEN

For My Digital Hero, Arfan
— from ATB

Little Hare Books
4/21 Mary Street, Surry Hills
NSW 2010 AUSTRALIA

First published in 2003

National Library of Australia
Cataloguing-in-Publication entry

Nilsen, Anna.
The amazeing voyage of Charles Darwin.

For children.
ISBN 1 877003 28 X.

1. Darwin, Charles, 1809-1882 - Juvenile literature. 2.
Maze puzzles - Juvenile literature. I. Title.

793.738

Designed by Louise McGeachie
Printed in Hong Kong
Produced by Phoenix Offset

2 4 5 3 1

It's an incredible journey!

Join Charles Darwin on an amazing voyage of discovery. In 1831, he set sail aboard the *Beagle* on a five-year scientific expedition from England to South America. As the ship's naturalist, Darwin studied plant and animal species—and his theories changed scientific thinking forever.

Be prepared for incredible sights! You'll see giant fossils of extinct animals, climb treacherous volcanoes and explore the wonders of the Galapagos Islands.

Start each maze at the green flag and find your way to the red flag. (Can't find the flags? Check their positions in the instructions box for each maze.) After you have returned safely to Plymouth at the end of the book, turn the page and find 12 extra puzzles to challenge your skills of observation.

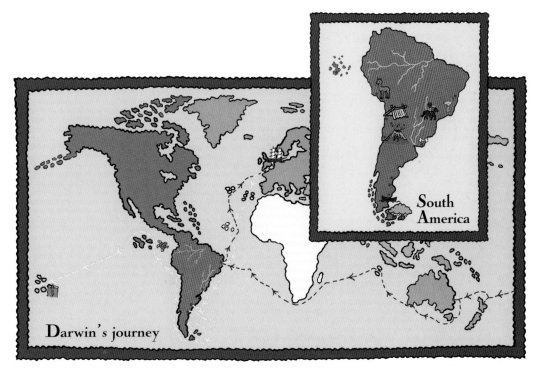

Darwin's journey

South America

Plymouth

Rio Negro

Punta Alta

Tapalguen

Santa Cruz

Tierra del Fuego

Chiloé

Concepción

The Andes

Galapagos Islands

Tahiti

Plymouth

All aboard! Help Darwin find his way to the *Beagle* so the voyage can begin.

Rio Negro

Scramble up the forest vines, then tread gently between the pink flamingos as you wade across the salt lake.

Punta Alta

Find a path from the ship to your tent, stepping carefully through the bone fossils littering the beach.

Tapalguen

Dodge the racing cowboys—and mind you don't get caught in a lasso!

Santa Cruz

Glide along the river's twisting currents
—but don't glide into a tapir!

Tierra del Fuego

Watch out for bolts of lightning as you island hop through stormy seas!

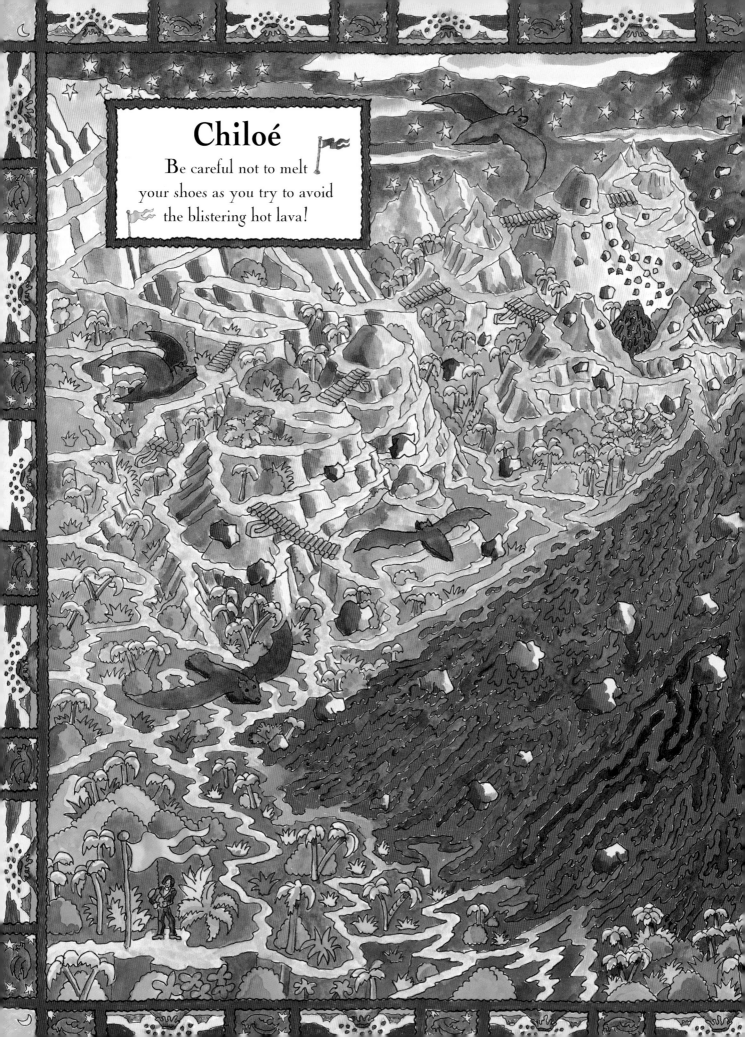

Chiloé

Be careful not to melt your shoes as you try to avoid the blistering hot lava!

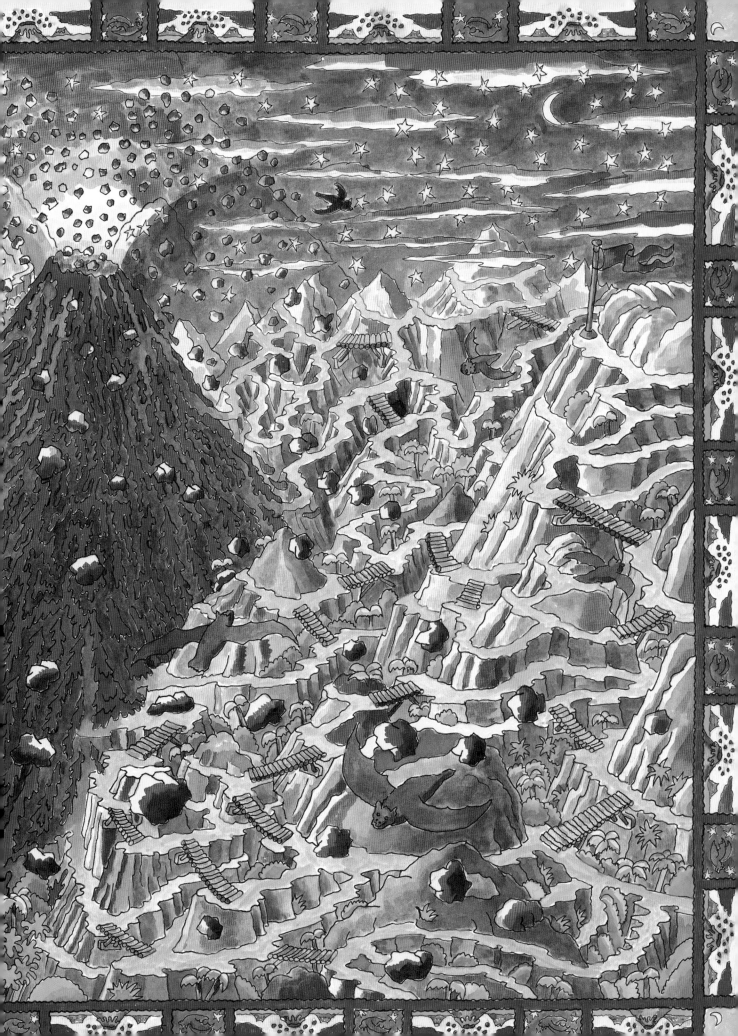

Concepción

Take care not to step on a crack in this town, which was devastated by an earthquake.

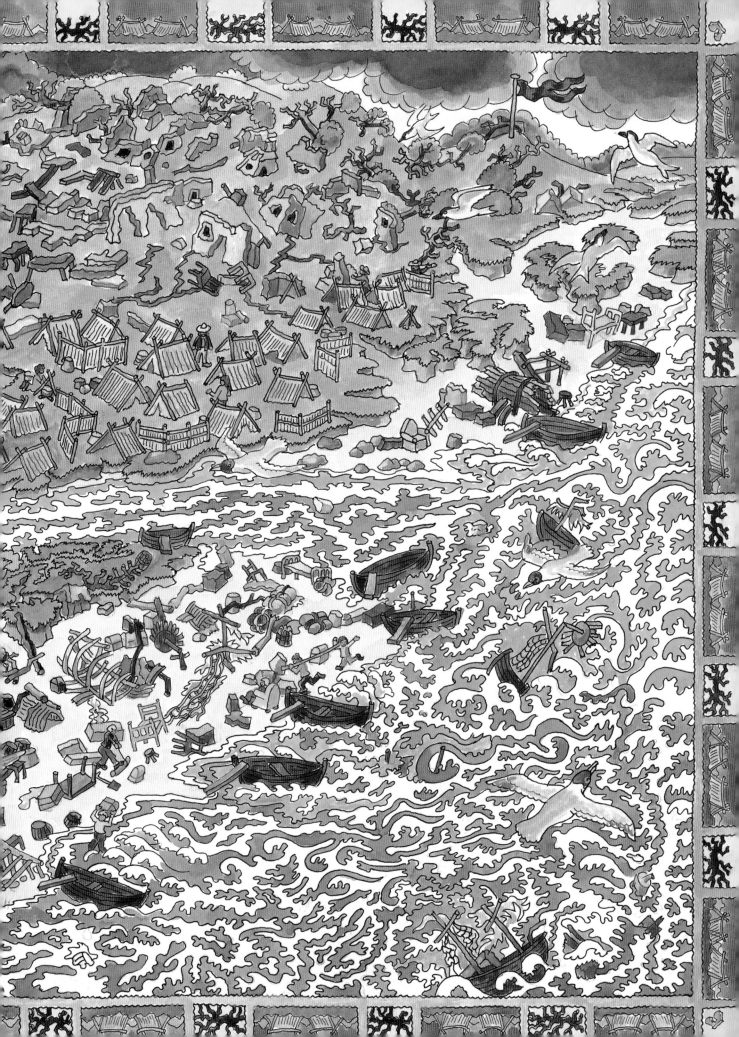

The Andes

Scale the highest peaks of the icy Andes.
You can use the guide ropes
to help you on the slippery slopes.

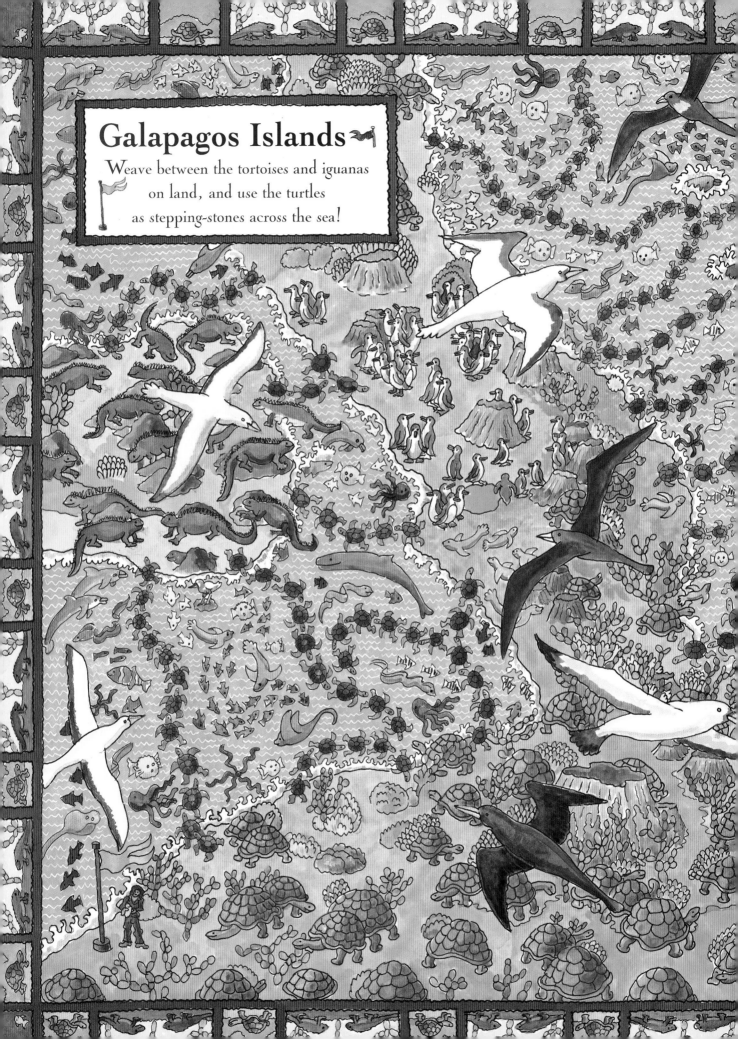

Galapagos Islands

Weave between the tortoises and iguanas
on land, and use the turtles
as stepping-stones across the sea!

Tahiti

Climb the cliffs of this tropical paradise, using the ropes to clamber from ledge to ledge.

The Journey Home

Follow the frothy waves halfway around the world on your journey home to Plymouth.

Puzzles

Now you be the naturalist! Test your observation skills with the following puzzles.

Plymouth

Can you find a microscope?

Rio Negro

Can you spot a green parrot?

Punta Alta

How many storm petrels can you find?

Tapalguen

Can you find a rhea?

Santa Cruz

How many cinammon teals can you see?

Tierra del Fuego

Can you find seven rufous-legged owls?

Chiloé
How many bats can you see?

Concepción
How many common terns can you spot?

Andes
Can you spot a puma?

Galapagos
Can you find five Darwin's finches?

Tahiti
How many superb fruit doves can you find?

Journey Home
How many kangaroos can you see?

Solutions!

These are the most direct routes through the mazes.

Rio Negro

Tapalguen

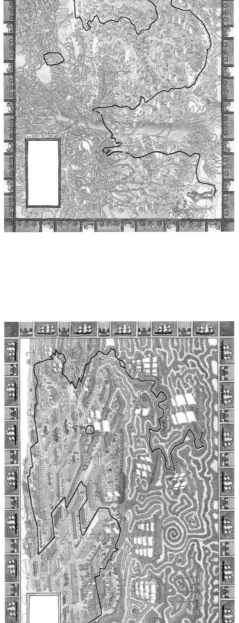

Plymouth

Punta Alta

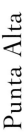

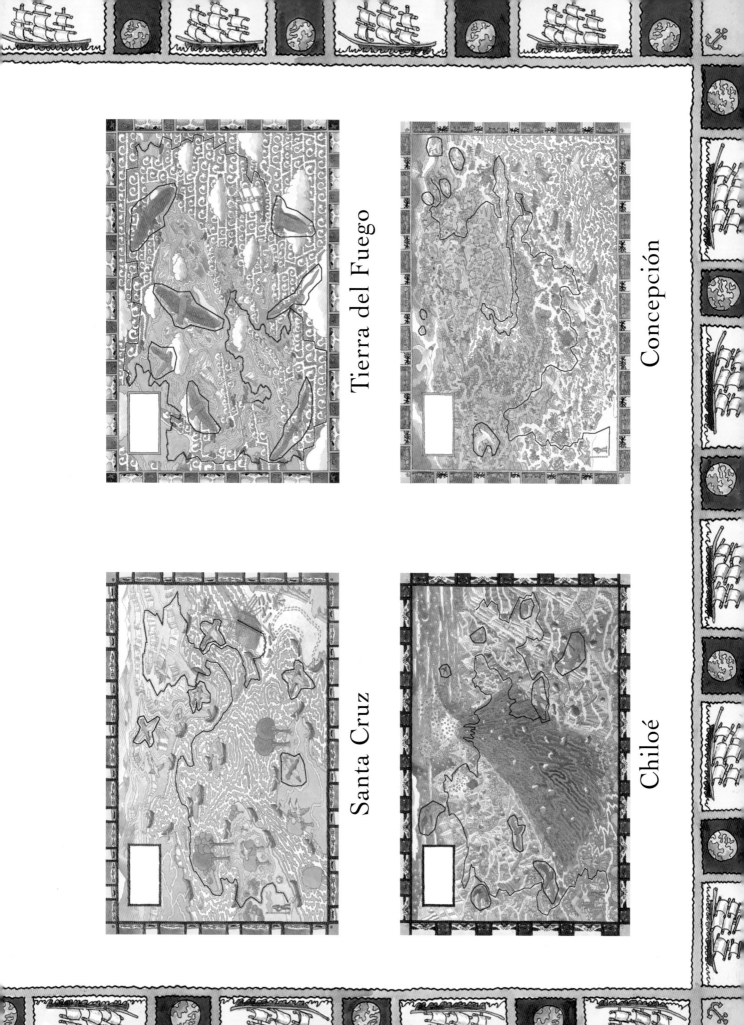

Tierra del Fuego

Concepción

Santa Cruz

Chiloé

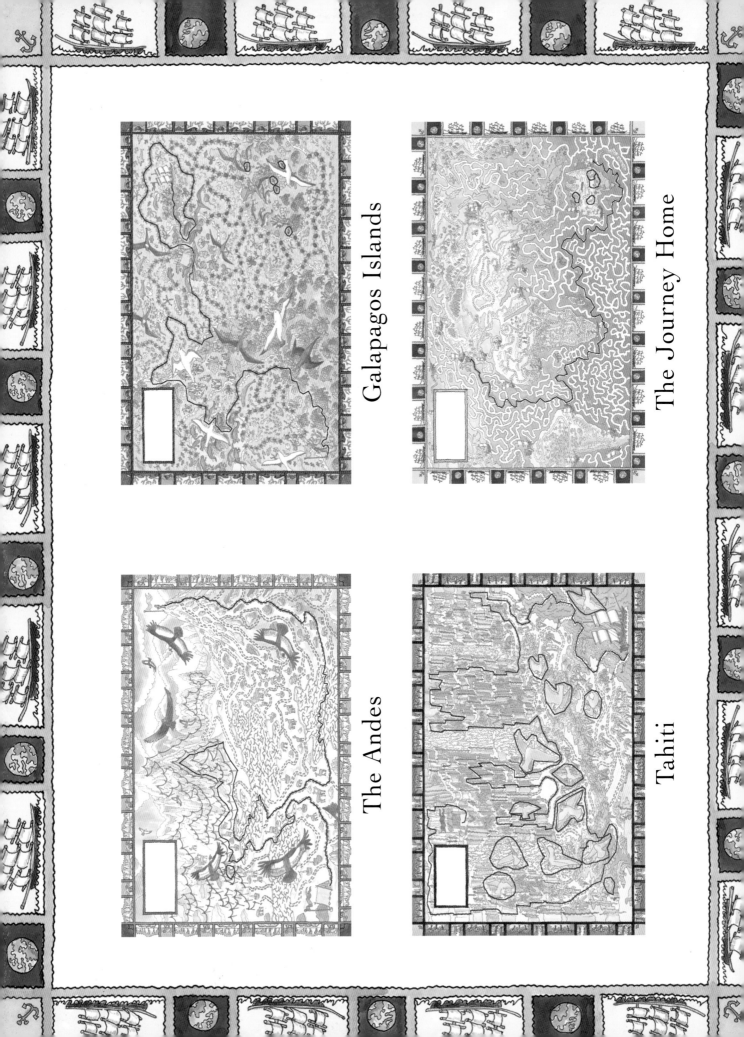

Galapagos Islands

The Journey Home

The Andes

Tahiti